The Long-Lost Coelacanth
and Other Living Fossils

This book is for Jason
and his friends Zander and Ethan

THE LONG-LOST COELACANTH
AND OTHER LIVING FOSSILS

WRITTEN AND ILLUSTRATED BY
ALIKI

Thomas Y. Crowell Company • New York

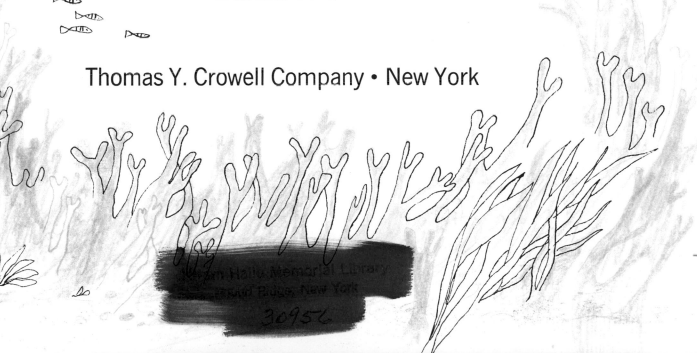

LET'S-READ-AND-FIND-OUT SCIENCE BOOKS

Editors: *DR. ROMA GANS*, Professor Emeritus of Childhood Education, Teachers College, Columbia University

DR. FRANKLYN M. BRANLEY, Chairman and Astronomer of The American Museum–Hayden Planetarium

*AVAILABLE IN SPANISH

Library of Congress Cataloging in Publication Data Aliki. The long-lost coelacanth. (Let's-read-and-find-out science book) SUMMARY: Describes the Coelacanth, a fish thought to have been extinct for seventy million years until one was discovered in 1938, and other examples of plants and animals known as "living fossils." 1. Coelacanth—Juvenile literature. 2. Living fossils—Juvenile literature. [1. Coelacanth. 2. Living fossils] I. Title. QL638.L26A44 597'.46 72-83773 ISBN 0-690-50478-0 ISBN 0-690-50479-9 (lib. bdg.)
1   2   3   4   5   6   7   8   9   10

The Long-Lost Coelacanth
and Other Living Fossils

One December day in 1938, a fisherman in South
   Africa caught a strange fish.
The fisherman had fished all his life.
But he had never seen a fish like this one.

1

The fish was almost five feet long.
It was a beautiful deep blue.
It was covered with large scales.
The strangest parts of the fish were its fins.
They did not lie flat the way most fins do.
They sprouted out of its body like paddles.

Little did the fisherman know that he had caught a
  wonderful present for scientists all over the world.

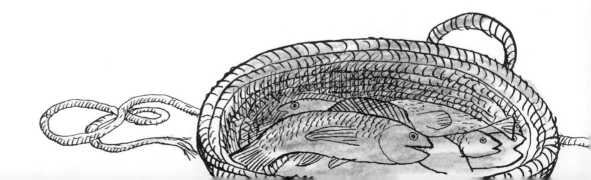

When scientists heard about the fish, they could not
   believe their ears.
They knew there had been fish like this 70 million
   years ago.
But they thought such fish had disappeared.
They thought they were extinct.
Yet, here was one of those ancient fish.
The fisherman had caught a COELACANTH!

Scientists knew about coelacanths.

They had found fossils of ancient coelacanths buried
  in stone.

Sometimes, when a coelacanth died, it was covered
  with mud.

In time, the mud became as hard as stone.

The fish became as hard as stone, too.

It became a fossil.

Scientists had studied coelacanth fossils.

This fossil of a coelacanth, buried in limestone,
  was found in Germany.
It shows that ancient coelacanths were much smaller
  than the one found in South Africa.

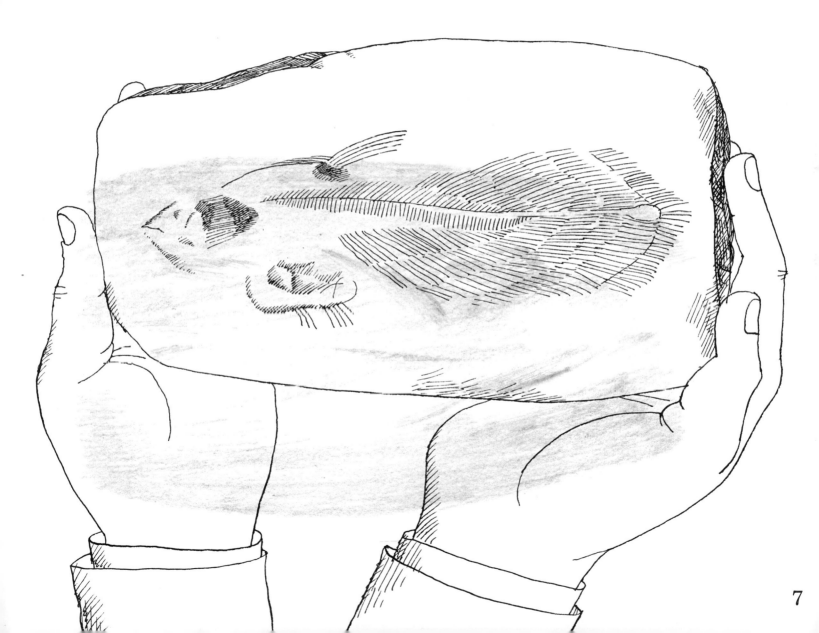

They knew the fish lived long ago.
They knew it was one of the first creatures to have a
  backbone.

TRILOBITE

NAUTILOID

Many creatures that were living long ago have died
out.
There are no live trilobites or nautiloids,
pteranodons or dinosaurs.
They are all extinct.
We can tell what they looked like because we have
found fossils of them.

PTERANODON

DINOSAUR
(Triceratops)

11

But some kinds of early animals and plants did not
  die out.
They did not become extinct.
We call them "living fossils" because they look very
  much like their ancestors, which lived millions of
  years ago.

Now a coelacanth had been found alive!
How excited the whole world was when the new
  "living fossil" was discovered.
People read about it in the newspapers.
Scientists knew there must be more coelacanths.
They put up posters, and offered a big reward to any
  fisherman who caught another one.

Fishermen fished and fished.
They looked and looked.
Even divers searched for coelacanths.

It took fourteen years to find another coelacanth.
Later, more were found.
About thirty coelacanths have been fished out of the
    sea.

Now scientists were able to study the fish and learn
    more about it.
They learned more about the past.

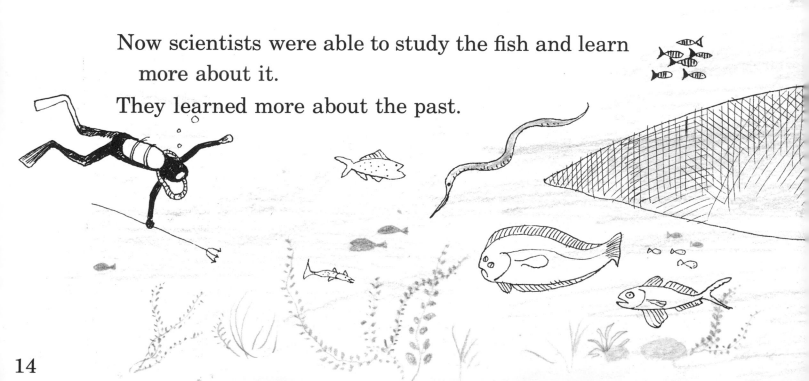

14

The coelacanth is a fish in the family of
crossopterygians.
Crossopterygians are different from all other fish.
They are the only fish with fins like paddles.
There are two groups of crossopterygians—the
coelacanths and the rhipidistians.

CROSSOPTERYGIANS
(means "fringe fin")

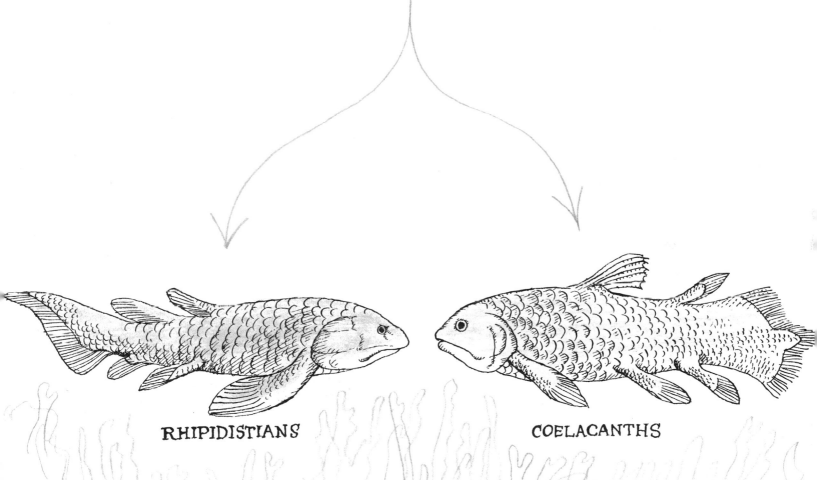

RHIPIDISTIANS

COELACANTHS

Scientists knew that when land began to form, some
　ancient fish grew legs.
The fish learned to breathe air, and to walk on dry
　land.
Scientists now know that the paddles of the crossopterygians
　were the start of legs.

The rhipidistians grew into the first amphibians.

Amphibians are animals that live on land as well as
   water.
Frogs and toads are amphibians.

But the coelacanth never lived on dry land.
It stayed in the water.
Its fins did not turn into legs.
The coelacanth looks just the way it did millions of
   years ago.
Only today it is bigger.

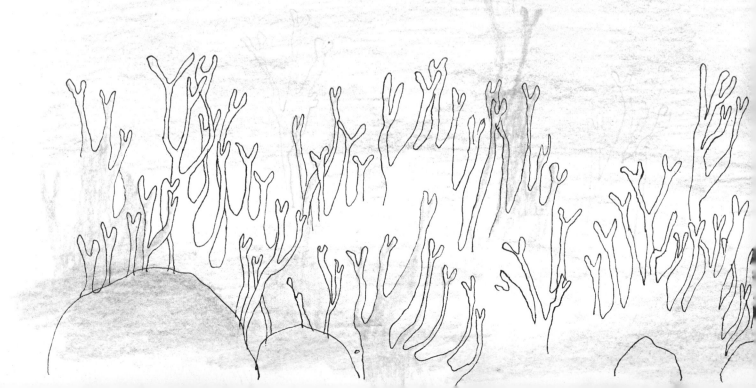

Some other living fossils have also changed in size
  or shape over the years.
Horses today are much bigger than they were.

EOHIPPUS WAS THE SIZE OF A FOX.

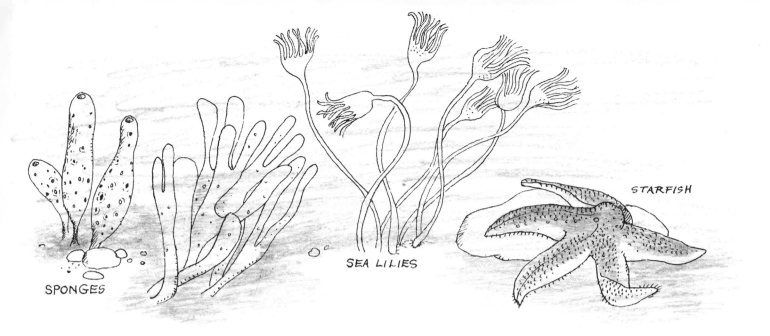

Still others have not changed.

Sponges, sea lilies, and starfish are animals that
    have lived in the sea for millions of years.

Yet they look the same now as they did long ago.

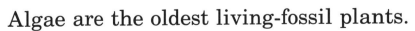

Algae are the oldest living-fossil plants.

They grow in water.

Algae have always been an important food for sea
    creatures.

The horseshoe crab has been crawling around for
    30 million years.
It is another living fossil.
The horseshoe crab has changed very little.

24

25

Dragonflies, cockroaches, and crocodiles are living
  fossils, too.
They have also changed.
Now they are much smaller than they used to be.

The tuatara is an ancient three-eyed lizard.
Its forefathers lived before the dinosaurs.
You cannot see the third eye of the tuatara.
It is in the middle of its forehead, covered with skin.

The Galapagos tortoise is enormous.
But fossils of ancient tortoises show that they were
once even bigger.

The funny-looking kiwi bird cannot fly.
Scientists are not sure if it is a living fossil.
They do not know what it looked like millions of
   years ago.
Perhaps one day a kiwi fossil will be found.
Then scientists will know the answer.

Perhaps the world may get another surprise some
  day.
There may be another living fossil hidden somewhere—
  one that we thought was extinct.
Imagine walking through a forest

and finding a live dinosaur!

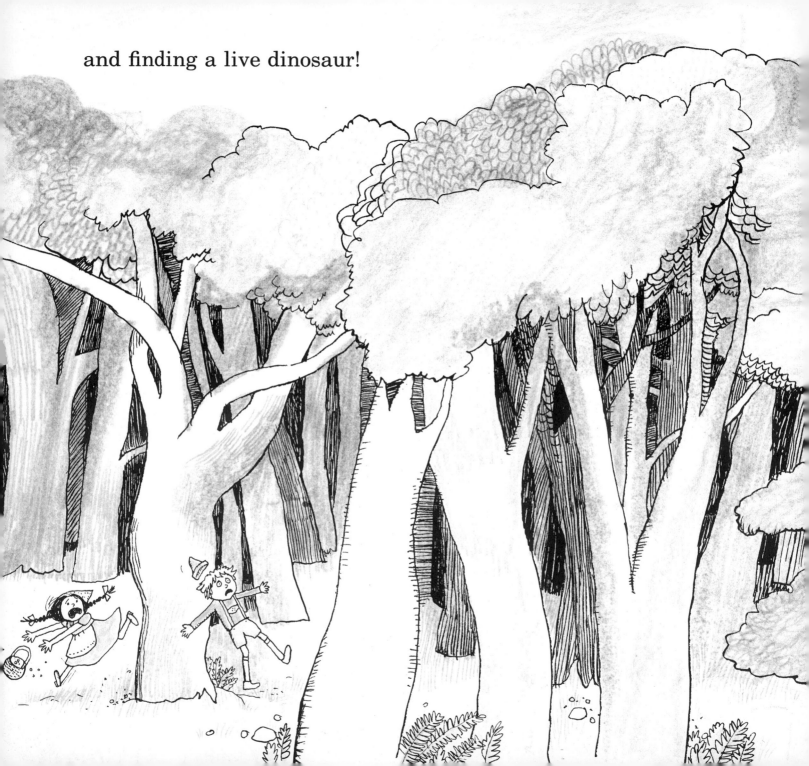

ABOUT THE AUTHOR-ILLUSTRATOR

Aliki worked in many phases of the art field before she began illustrating and writing children's books. Now, when she is not too busy with books, she makes puppets and scenery for the family puppet theater, weaves baskets, and macramés.

Aliki Brandenberg grew up in Philadelphia and graduated from the Museum College of Art. She has traveled to many countries with her husband, Franz Brandenberg, and their children, Jason and Alexa. They now live in New York City.

Aliki and her family are familiar with many kinds of living fossils. Some they collect and exhibit.

Others, they do not.